Schaum Fingerpower Pop

PRIMER

10 PIANO SOLOS WITH TECHNIQUE WARM-UPS

Arranged by JAMES POTEAT

The purpose of the Fingerpower Pop series is to provide musical experiences beyond the traditional **Fingerpower®** books. The series offers students a variety of popular tunes, including hits from today's pop charts as well as classic movie themes, beloved Broadway shows, and more! The arrangements progress in order of difficulty, and many include optional accompaniments. In addition, technique warm-ups precede each pop solo.

CONTENTS

3	Heigh-Ho	13	Happy Birthday to You
5	Iron Man	15	Supercalifra...
7	Over the Rainbow	17	Castle or
9	You've Got a Friend in Me	20	All of Me
11	You Are My Sunshine	22	Peter Cotto...

ISBN 978-1-4950-9763-8

Schaum

EXCLUSIVELY DISTRIBUTED BY

HAL•LEONARD®

7777 W. BLUEMOUND RD. P.O. BOX 13819 MILWAUKEE, WI 53213

Visit Hal Leonard Online at
www.halleonard.com

Warm-Ups

1. STACCATO 2nds

2. STACCATO 3rds

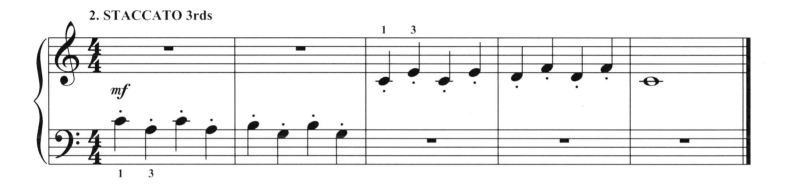

3. LEGATO 2nds

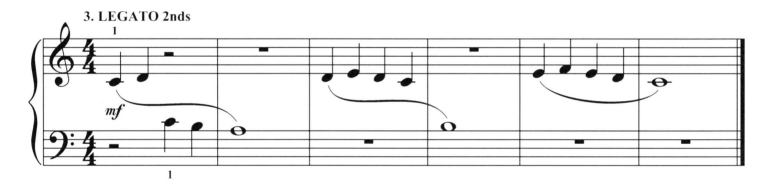

HEIGH-HO | Accompaniment (Student plays one octave higher than written.)

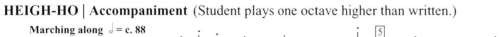

Heigh-Ho
The Dwarfs' Marching Song from SNOW WHITE AND THE SEVEN DWARFS

Words by Larry Morey
Music by Frank Churchill

Marching along ♩ = c. 88

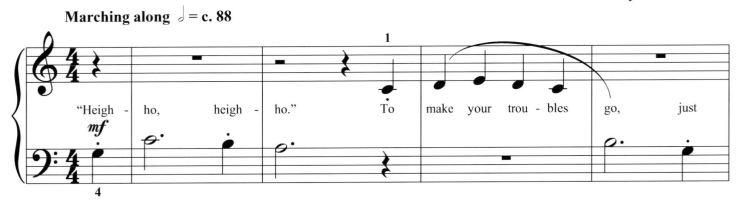

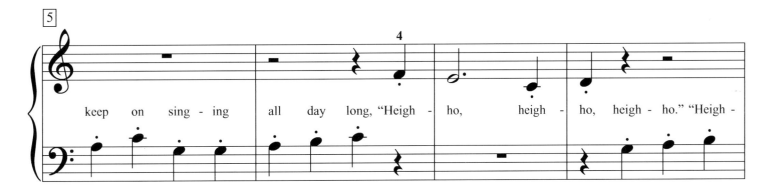

Warm-Ups

1. TWO-NOTE SLURS

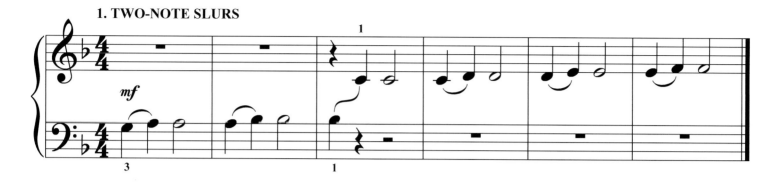

2. IRON FINGERS

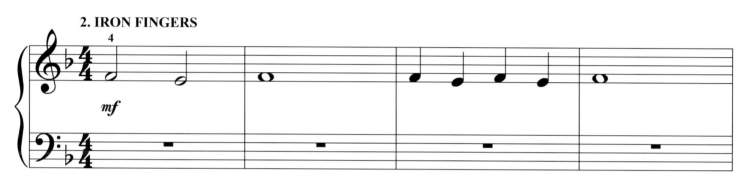

IRON MAN | Accompaniment (Student plays one octave higher than written.)

Iron Man

Words and Music by Frank Iommi,
John Osbourne, William Ward
and Terence Butler
Arranged by James Poteat

Warm-Ups

1. THUMB TRADE-OFF

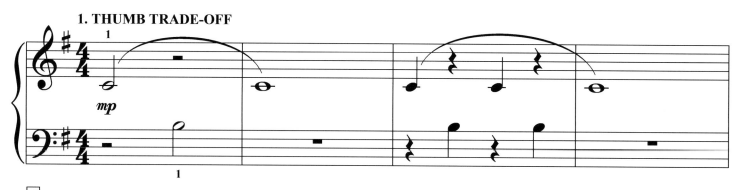

2. 3rds & 2nds IN SEQUENCE

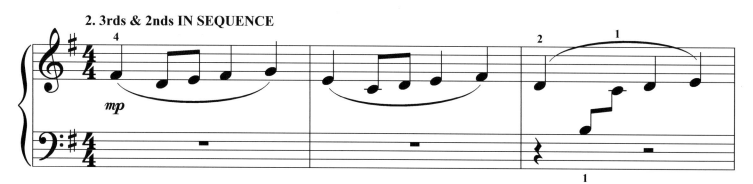

OVER THE RAINBOW | Accompaniment (Student plays **two** octaves higher than written.)

Over the Rainbow
from THE WIZARD OF OZ

Music by Harold Arlen
Lyric by E.Y. "Yip" Harburg
Arranged by James Poteat

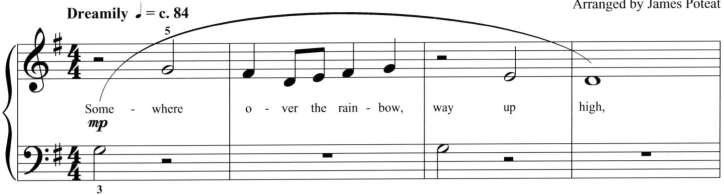

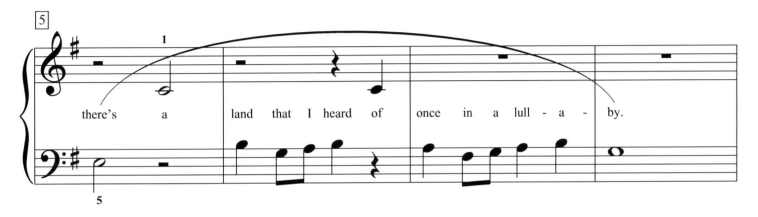

Warm-Ups

1. LEGATO 2nds

2. 3rds IN SEQUENCE

YOU'VE GOT A FRIEND IN ME | Accompaniment (Student plays one octave higher than written.)

Cheerfully ♩ = c. 112

You've Got a Friend in Me

from TOY STORY

Music and Lyrics by
Randy Newman
Arranged by James Poteat

Cheerfully ♩ = c. 112*

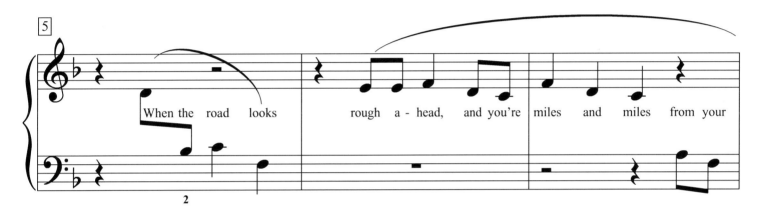

*Optional: swing eighths

Warm-Ups

1. LEGATO 2nds (4/4)

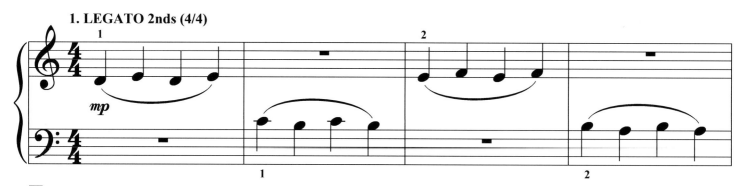

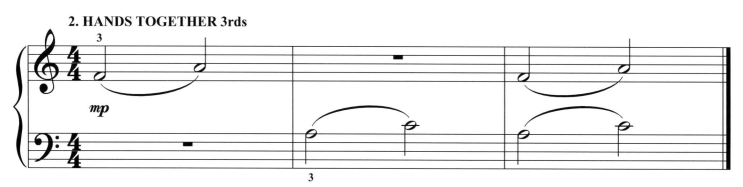

2. HANDS TOGETHER 3rds

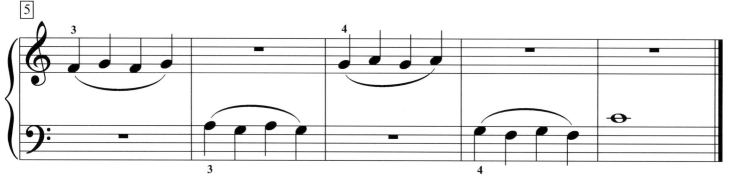

3. HANDS TOGETHER 2nds

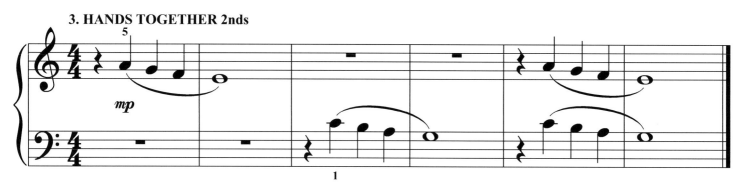

YOU ARE MY SUNSHINE | Accompaniment (Student plays one octave higher than written.)

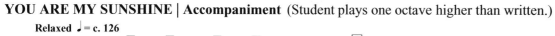

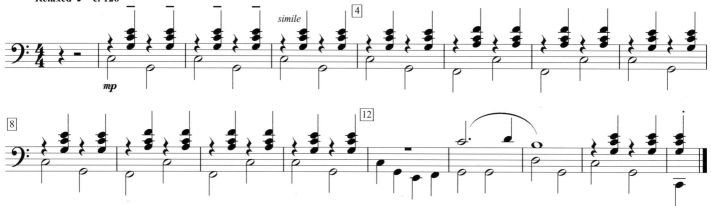

You Are My Sunshine

Words and Music by
Jimmie Davis
Arranged by James Poteat

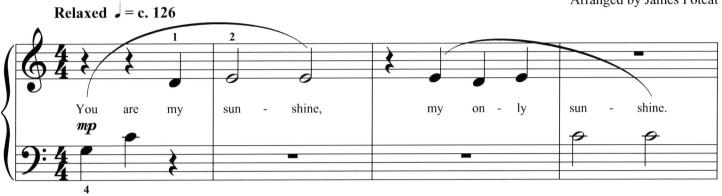

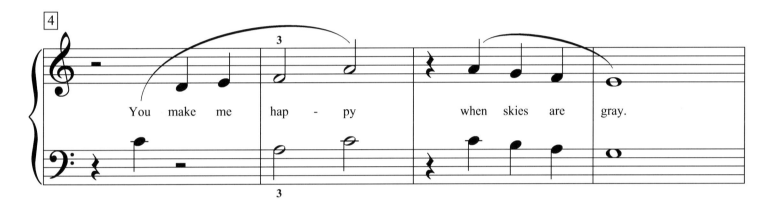

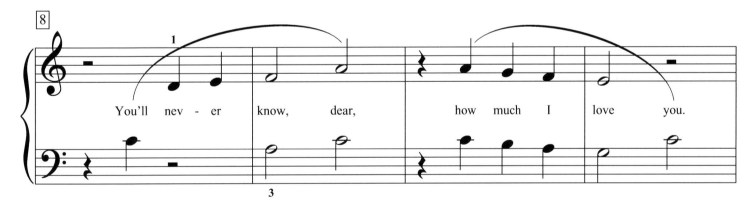

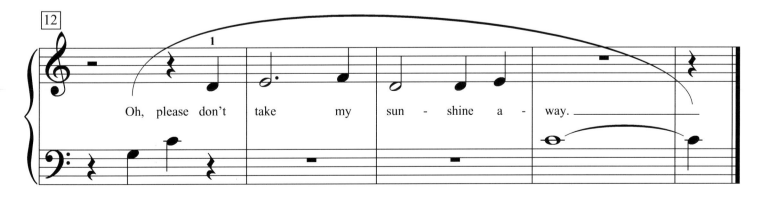

Warm-Up

LEGATO 2nds (3/4)

mf

3

5

1

2

9

3

13

5

4

HAPPY BIRTHDAY TO YOU | Accompaniment (Student plays one octave higher than written.)

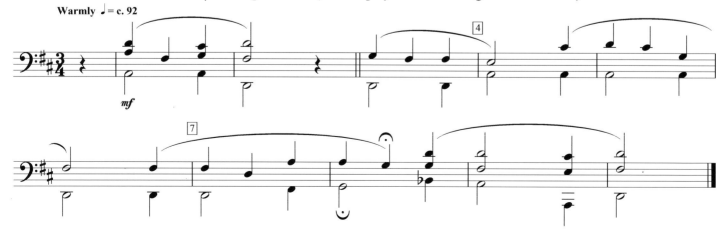

Warmly ♩ = c. 92

mf

4

7

Happy Birthday to You

Words and Music by Mildred J. Hill
and Patty S. Hill
Arranged by James Poteat

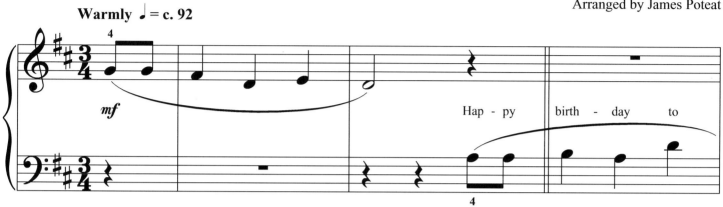

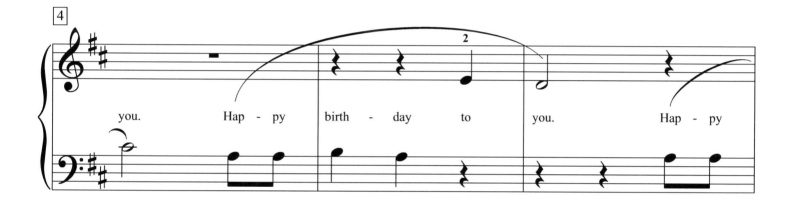

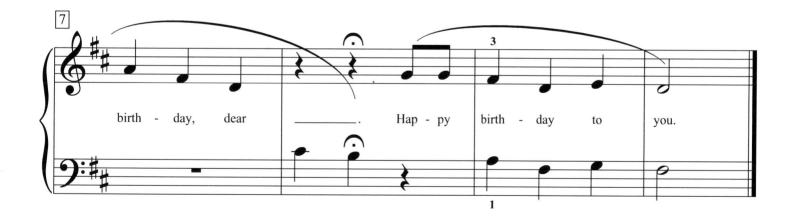

Warm-Ups

1. SLURRING TO C

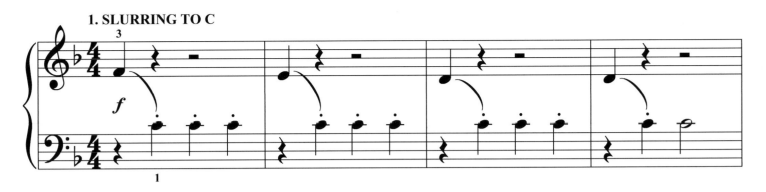

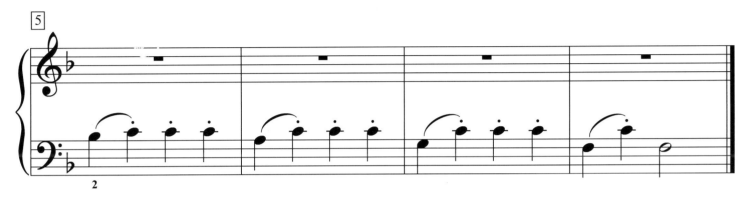

2. THE BIG FINISH! (Watch the fingering)

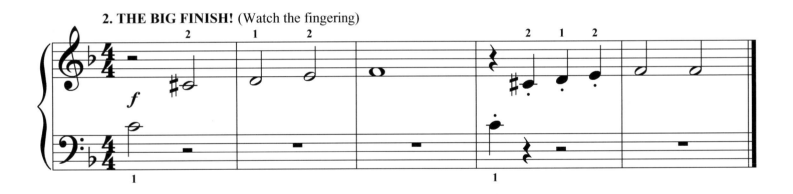

SUPERCALIFRAGILISTICEXPIALIDOCIOUS | Accompaniment (Student plays one octave higher than written.)

Supercalifragilisticexpialidocious

from MARY POPPINS

Words and Music by Richard M. Sherman
and Robert B. Sherman
Arranged by James Poteat

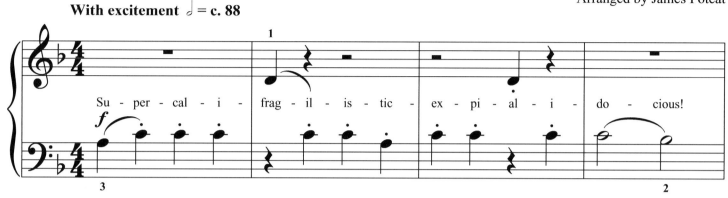

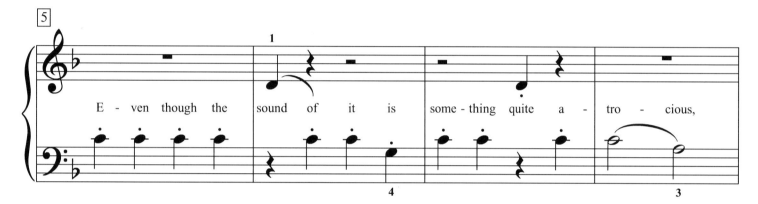

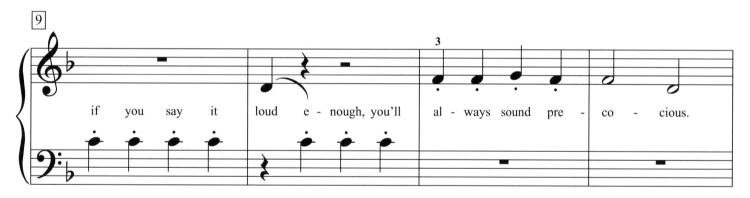

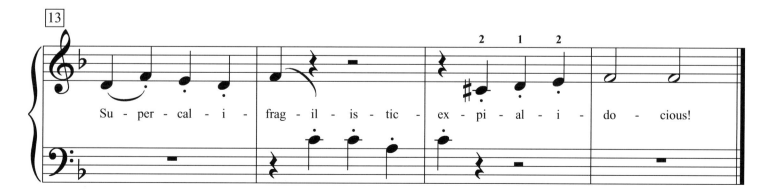

Warm-Ups

1. PARALLEL 2nds

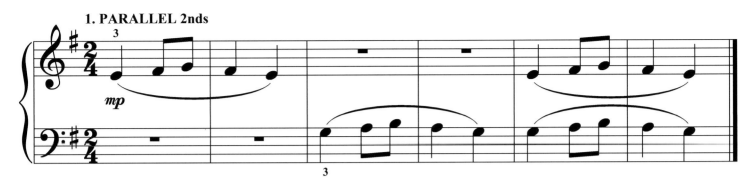

2. 5-FINGER LEGATO

3. THUMB TRADE-OFF

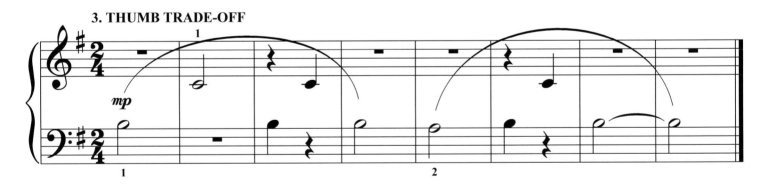

CASTLE ON A CLOUD | Accompaniment (Student plays one octave higher than written.)

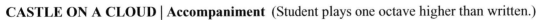

Castle on a Cloud
from Les Misérables

Music by Claude-Michel Schönberg
Lyrics by Alain Boublil,
Jean-Marc Natel and Herbert Kretzmer
Arranged by James Poteat

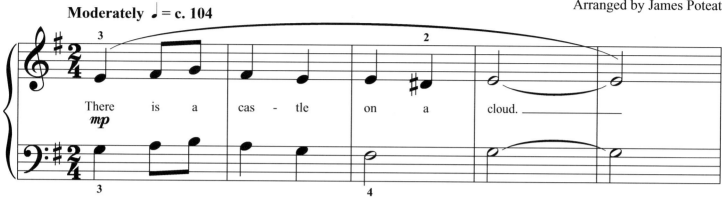

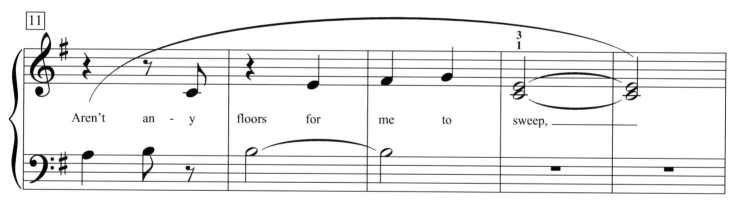

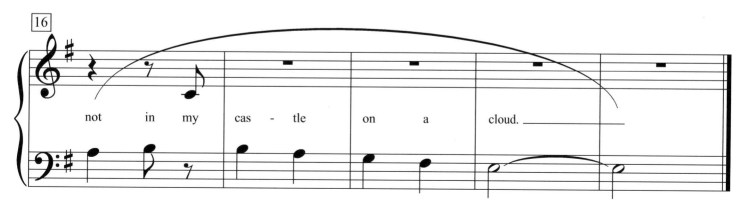

Warm-Ups for "All of Me"
(page 20)

1. ALTERNATING HANDS

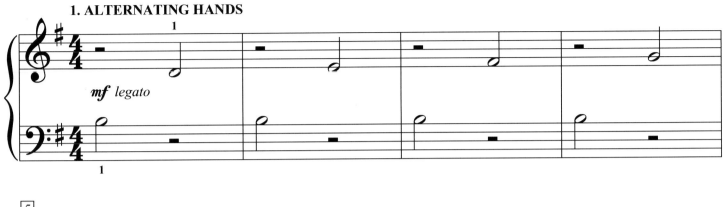

⑤

2. MOVING THE LEFT HAND

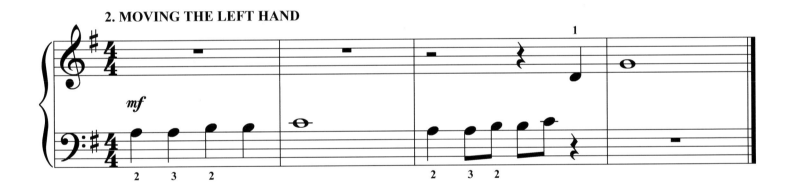

3. PARALLEL 2nds

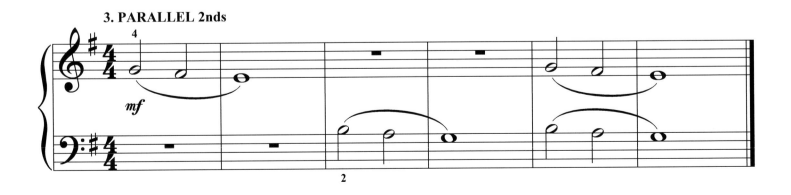

Warm-Ups for "Peter Cottontail"

(page 22)

1. HOPPING 2nds

2. HOPPING 3rds

All of Me

Words and Music by John Stephens
and Toby Gad
Arranged by James Poteat

Accompaniment (Student plays one octave higher than written.)

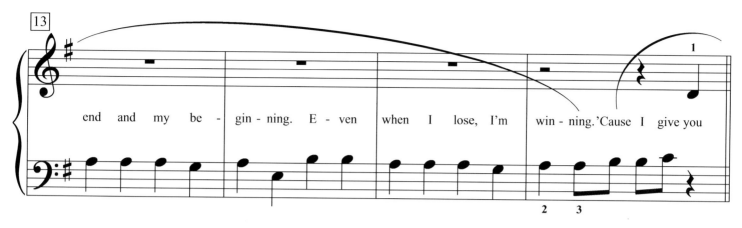

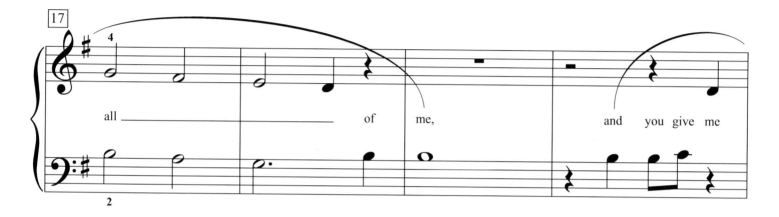

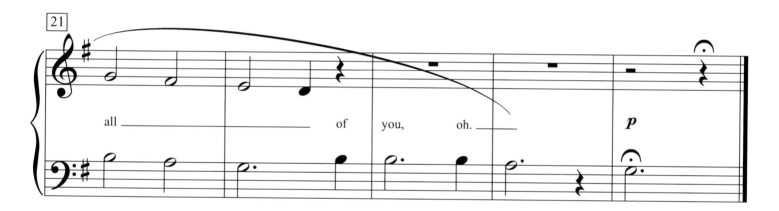

Peter Cottontail

Words and Music by Steve Nelson
and Jack Rollins
Arranged by James Poteat

Accompaniment (Student plays one octave higher than written.)

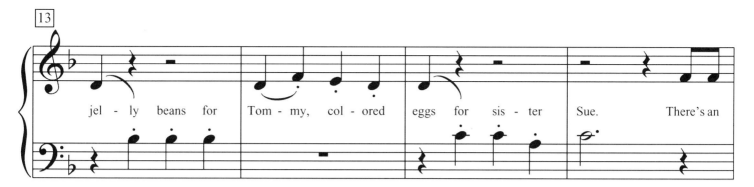

jel - ly beans for Tom - my, col - ored eggs for sis - ter Sue. There's an

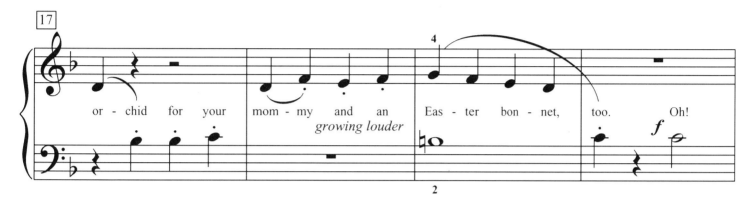

or - chid for your mom - my and an Eas - ter bon - net, too. Oh!

growing louder

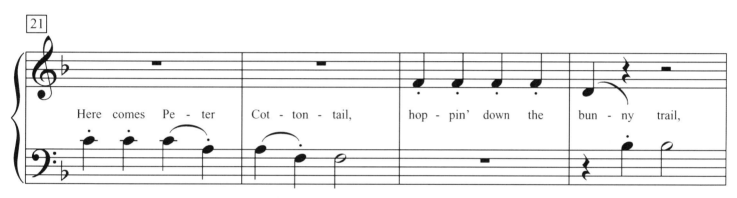

Here comes Pe - ter Cot - ton - tail, hop - pin' down the bun - ny trail,

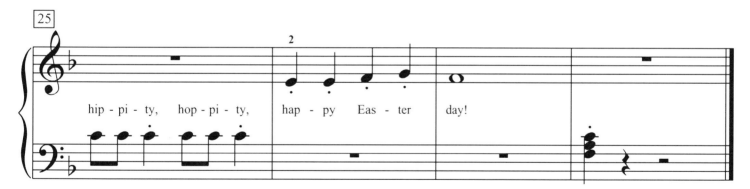

hip - pi - ty, hop - pi - ty, hap - py Eas - ter day!

ALSO AVAILABLE

Fingerpower Pop – Level One
Arranged by JAMES POTEAT
Mid to Late Elementary
HL00237510

10 great piano solos with technique warm-ups! Includes: Hallelujah • Lean on Me • Let's Go Fly a Kite • Once Upon a Dream • Reindeer(s) Are Better Than People • Shake It Off • Somewhere Out There • Take Me Out to the Ball Game • We're Off to See the Wizard • Yellow Submarine.

ABOUT THE ARRANGER

Since 2007 **James Poteat** has taught piano, trombone, euphonium, music theory, and composition in Woodstock, Georgia. Mr. Poteat works with students of all ages and skill levels and is equally comfortable in the worlds of popular and classical music. James is constantly arranging music for his students and is dedicated to creating and using materials of the highest quality. Learn more about James and his work by visiting **www.musicalintentions.com**.
